vintage christmas landscape

vintage christmas
coloring book

LIVING ART
Vintage

Copyright © 2020 Living Art Vintage

Christmas
adult coloring books for women

Vintage Mom
coloring books for adults

Kitchen Life

grayscale coloring books for adults

LIVING ART Vintage

www.ingramcontent.com/pod-product-compliance
Lightning Source LLC
LaVergne TN
LVHW060220080526
838202LV00052B/4312